Caring For Your Cat

by Mark McPherson

photography by
Marianne Bernstein

Troll Associates

Library of Congress Cataloging in Publication Data

McPherson, Mark (Mark D.)
  Caring for your cat.

  Includes index.
  Summary: An illustrated guide to caring for and
raising a kitten as a pet. Includes information on
selection, feeding, housebreaking, and training.
  1. Cats—Juvenile literature. [1. Cats] I. Bernstein,
Marianne, ill. II. Title.
SF445.7.M33   1984   636.8   84-223
ISBN 0-8167-0115-6 (lib. bdg.)
ISBN 0-8167-0116-4 (pbk.)

The author and publisher wish to thank the ASPCA of New York, the Animal Medical Center of New York, Hillary
Jurman, Laura and Alexander Spelman, and all of our other good friends and cats.

Principal photography by Marianne Bernstein: cover, and pages 4, 12 (top), 16, 18, 19, 20, 21, 22, 24, 26, 27, 28,
29, 32, 34, 36, and 42. Photographs on pages 10, 12 (bottom), 13, 14 (bottom) by Jane Howard; pages 14 (top),
15, 38, 41 by Crezentia Allen; page 6 by Michael Mauney; page 8 by David White.

Contents

Getting to Know Cats

Cats are one of the most independent, graceful, and beautiful of animals. They are also one of the most popular pets. While cats do not usually display the same kind of affection and loyalty shown by dogs, cats are far easier to raise, train, and care for.

Cats are natural hunters and belong to the same family as the tiger and the lion, the king of the jungle.

Keeping a house cat is a tradition that can be traced to as far back as ancient Egypt. The Egyptians prized cats for their beauty and character.

Besides their value as companions, cats have contributed a great service to civilization. Cats are natural hunters of mice and rats. Throughout history, they have helped to rid homes, towns, and cities of these unwanted rodents. This was—and still is—important, because wild rodents carry diseases and harm food supplies.

Part of a cat's hunting skill depends on its ability to move about at night. One theory says that this ability is aided by a cat's whiskers, which are really delicate sense organs. The whiskers of a cat are extremely sensitive to touch. Each time they touch an object, the cat blinks. This may mean that they are an early warning system that helps protect the cat's eyes.

But whiskers are only part of the story. A cat's nighttime vision is far superior to our own. A cat can easily pick up the movements of a busy mouse scurrying under the cover of darkness.

The king of the jungle is a member of the cat family.

In folklore, cats have been a source of mystery and superstition. In many parts of Great Britain, a black cat crossing one's path was a sign of good luck. In North and South America, however, a black cat was a sign of bad luck. Black cats also remind us of witches, especially on Halloween. And for centuries, many people have watched the behavior of cats in order to predict what the weather will be. For instance, some say that rain is on the way when a cat washes its face.

All of these superstitions may be the result of the way cats act. Cats often look as though they know something that the rest of us do not. If you stare into a cat's eyes, you will get a sense of distance. You may see why people consider them mysterious creatures.

Dogs are often called "man's best friend," in part because they almost always respond enthusiastically to any attention their owners might give them. Cats, on the other hand, often resist your efforts to pet them or show them affection. Yet at other times they will come to you on their own and rub their ears against your ankles.

Cats will frequently come when you call them, but you cannot expect them to sit or stay on command the way dogs do. They will, however, learn the sounds associated with feeding. The banging of a certain cabinet or the sound of their dish being lightly rapped on the floor will bring cats running to you. With patience, you can teach a cat to perform some tricks. You can teach your cat to sit if you use a treat as a bribe.

Mystery and superstition have followed cats through history.

Cats often look and act as though they are above it all.

Most cats are exceptional at keeping themselves clean and well-groomed. They clean themselves after meals. Their self-grooming is important, because most of them dislike water and baths.

Cats are rarely shy about expressing their moods. If something annoys a cat, like someone scratching its back when it absolutely wants to be left alone, it will take a quick swipe at the offending hand with its paw.

Many people become attached and devoted to their cats. A good cat owner will respect his or her cat's moods and daily routines. Cat lovers often have two—or more—pet cats. The average life span of a cat is twelve years, but with recent improvements in veterinary care, some cats are living much longer.

If you want to become a cat owner, too, you first must decide what kind of cat you want.

2

The Different Kinds of Cats

Cats come in many varieties. Most are "mixed" breeds, meaning that they are a combination of two or more "pure" breeds, or types. "Pure" breeds, or purebreds, are cats that are born as the result of a mating between two cats of the same breed. A Siamese (a popular purebred cat) is, for example, the offspring of two Siamese parents.

Mixed breeds can be just as beautiful and intelligent as purebreds. But mixed-breed cats will not have the distinctive features that purebreds have.

Most cats belong to one of two basic types: shorthairs and longhairs. With one possible exception, neither type of cat is better to own. The possible exception is that shorthairs need only a moderate amount of brushing. Longhairs, on the other hand, need a lot of brushing.

Shorthairs may have fur of only one color. Or they may have a mixture of several different colors. The American Shorthair, the most common shorthair type, includes the beautiful tabby cat.

Other cats in the shorthair category are Siamese, Abyssinian, Burmese, and Manx. The Manx cat is famous for often having no tail.

Longhairs: The Persian cat is the most common longhair, and it can be one of as many as forty colors. There is even a longhair cat with tabby markings.

This purebred Somali has a fluffy tail.

Kittens of all kinds love adventure.

An Abyssinian has a proud, ancient-looking appearance.

Other types of longhairs are the Balinese, the Himalayan, and the Maine Coon Cat, which is a big cat that often weighs over fifteen pounds.

Most pet cats are probably mixtures of two or more of these breeds. People are usually eager to give away these mixed breeds. The purebreds, however, can cost a great deal of money, especially if you want to enter them in cat shows.

It's true. Most Manx cats do not have tails.

Persian longhairs need regular amounts of brushing.

The Himalayan looks a bit grouchy, but it really has an easy-going temperament.

The Maine Coon is a big, friendly cat that often weighs fifteen pounds or more.

Some cat lovers take little interest in purebreds. Instead, they search for kittens that are unique and beautiful in appearance. But this is all a matter of personal taste. The important thing is to have a cat that you like and to give it the care and love it needs.

3

Your New Kitten

The first step toward having a good pet cat is choosing a healthy kitten. Visit a litter of kittens about two weeks before they are ready to leave their mother. They will be six weeks old. Ask permission to pick up the kittens, and be very gentle when you do so.

Make sure that a kitten has clear, bright eyes and a shiny, full coat. Check the skin under the fur for any problems such as sores, rashes, or bald spots. You want to choose a kitten that has healthy skin.

Next, make sure that the kitten is neither too thin nor too fat. A kitten that is either all skin and bones or has a bloated belly is likely to have an infection. Do not select such a kitten. Also check the kitten's nose and ears for any sign of discharge or infection.

While you are checking for signs of physical health, take note of the kitten's temperament. Carry the kitten to another part of the room and watch how it behaves. Is it nervous or scared? Does it respond to gentle petting by growing calmer? You want a kitten that adjusts quickly to you. This is a sign that it has been handled by the owners of the litter, which is important in preparing the kitten for living with people.

It is extremely important to start out with a friendly cat. A scratching, hissing, or terribly frightened kitten will grow up to be a difficult cat at best. At worst, the kitten will never become a friendly, loving pet.

After you have chosen a kitten that you like, make arrangements to pick it up when it is ready to leave its mother (when it is about eight weeks old). A day or two 17

Check the newspaper classified ads under "Pets" for notices of free kittens.

after you get your new kitten, take it to a veterinarian (an animal doctor). The vet will give it the first in a series of shots to protect it against common cat diseases. Tell the vet if you intend to let the cat outdoors. If you do intend to let it out, the kitten may need a shot to protect it against rabies.

The vet will also examine the kitten for signs of disease. Bring along a sample of the kitten's droppings so that the doctor can check for worms.

If the vet gives you medicine for the kitten, make sure that you or one of your parents understand how to give the medicine. Ask the vet or the vet's assistant to show you the proper method. Give the medicine to the kitten *exactly* as directed by the vet. Twice a day is not good enough if the kitten is supposed to get medicine three times a day.

Young kittens like to eat every few hours, about four times a day. At each meal, serve a saucer of fresh milk alongside a small dish of dry cat food. For one or two of the meals, mix in canned cat food (meat or fish). If the kitten gets diarrhea, switch to powdered milk. If the diarrhea continues, reduce the amount of milk and the number of meals at which it is served.

Kittens love occasional treats, such as fresh liver, kidney, or cottage cheese. But dry cat food is the best thing for a steady diet. Keep treats to once or twice a week.

As the kitten grows older, you can gradually reduce the number of meals. At six months, two meals each day are adequate. At one year, one meal a day is all that is needed. If your cat pesters you for a second meal, give a little more than half of the one-meal portion twice a day. The size of portions is usually recommended on the cat food box.

For your new kitten, and later your adult cat, keep a bowl filled with fresh water at all times.

An alert, lively kitten is likely to make a good pet.

19

Kittens take their cat naps whenever and wherever they like.

Although your kitten will decide for itself where it will sleep, it might enjoy a soft, snug spot you prepare for it. A fluffy, clean hand towel, folded and placed in a shoe box that sits on its side, could make an attractive bed for your kitten. But the kitten may just decide to perch itself on a chair instead.

You will have to help your kitten get used to using a litter box to go to the bathroom. Getting your cat used to a litter box is usually easy, because cats are naturally clean and like to bury their droppings. A litter box is nothing more than a shallow rectangular container. The easiest kind to use is made of soft plastic. Into this you pour cat litter, which is sold in stores. Cover the bottom of the litter box with about two inches of cat litter.

20

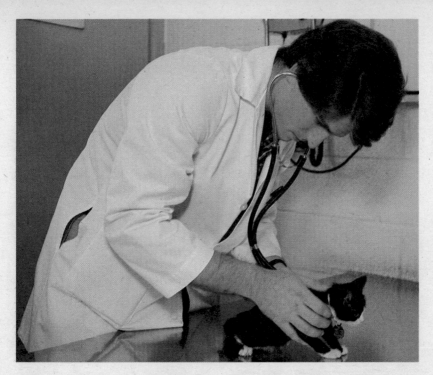

Have your new kitten checked by a veterinarian the first week you bring it home.

A young cat enjoys a mixture of dry and canned cat food.

Take your kitten to its litter box as soon as you bring it home. Sometimes that first visit is all that is needed. But until you are sure that the kitten understands, take it there after each feeding.

Sometimes cats will not use a litter box if something about the particular brand of litter is not to their liking. Occasionally they will avoid the box if its location is not private enough. Try to solve these problems if the kitten does not use the litter box from the start.

About the only unpleasant task involved in owning a cat is cleaning the litter box every two or three days. If you do not clean it, the box will begin to smell.

Empty all the used litter into a paper or plastic bag and take it outside to the garbage. Then wash the litter box with soap and water. Put the newly filled box back in the same place, so that you do not upset your cat's routine.

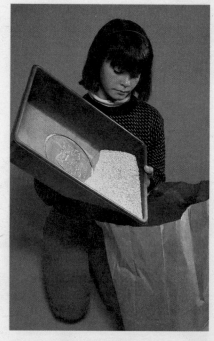

Introduce your kitten to its litter box as soon as you bring it home.

Empty the litter box regularly.

If you plan on allowing your cat to go outside, you may decide to let it go to the bathroom outdoors. In this case, do not provide a litter box. Instead, take your new kitten outdoors to a spot where there is a patch of dirt in which it can dig and bury. After a few days, the kitten will wait by the door to be let out. Some people even install little cat doors so that their pets can come and go as they please.

An outdoor cat should wear a collar with an identification tag on it. The tag should give the cat's name as well as your name and address.

Now that you know how to make your kitten feel welcome in its new home, it is time for you and your kitten to get to know one another.

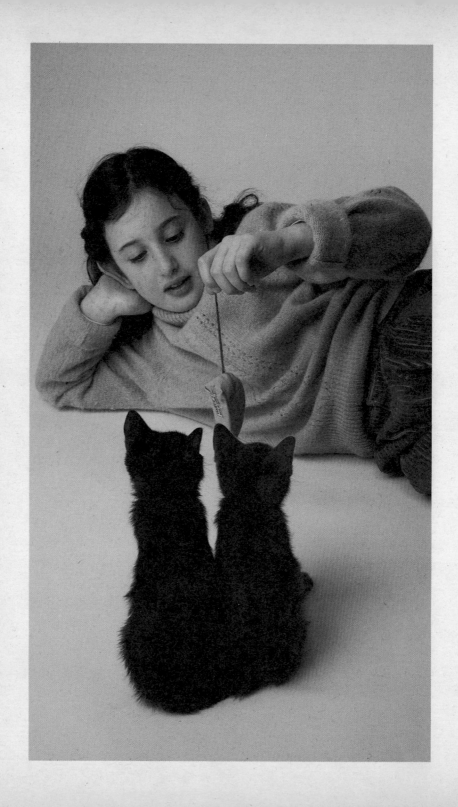

4

Getting to Know Your Kitten

For a kitten to grow into a friendly pet cat, you must hold and play with it a great deal. Otherwise, the kitten might keep to itself and grow up without getting used to your attention and affection.

Your kitten needs to be held and petted as often as possible. Hold it by placing one hand under its chest, while using your other hand to steady the kitten and give it a sense of security. Try to pet it gently and hold it until it begins to purr, which is a sign of great contentment.

You should also get down on the floor and invite the kitten to play. Drum your fingers on the floor to attract the kitten's attention. Soon it will pounce on your hand. During this kind of play, the kitten is practicing its hunting skills. Be careful not to let the cat scratch or bite you.

Your kitten will also enjoy chasing or wrestling with any object tied to a string and dangled in front of it. If you have never known a kitten before, you may be surprised and fascinated by how long and energetically the kitten will play this game.

Do not forget to invite other people to play with your kitten. This will encourage your pet to be friendly to all people and to accept their affection. If you enjoy your cat, you will probably want others to share that enjoyment.

Cats do not really take well to discipline of any kind. Because they are so independent, most of the time they will do as they please. Cats do accept love and affec-

Getting down on the floor to play with your kitten will help it get used to people.

tion from you, and they also return it. But they could just as easily do without it.

Remember that cats are excellent hunters and can fend for themselves out in the world. Shouting at them and hitting them, for any reason, might make them decide to run away.

Part of your job as a cat owner is to learn your cat's ways, its likes and dislikes. Your cat may, for instance, like to play energetically for a while and then be left alone while it naps. It will probably seek a sunny windowsill for one of its nap spots. So unless you have something else in that area, like plants, you should respect your cat's choice.

In other words, your cat will establish its own style of living. You should attempt to change that style only if it is necessary.

One area in which you must be firm is feeding. If you allow them to, cats frequently become fussy eaters. Preventing fussiness is another good reason to get cats used to basic, dry cat food. Many experts agree that dry food is the most balanced and wholesome meal a cat can eat. A cat can be spoiled by being fed too many treats, such as liver and kidney, or even too much canned food. So establish a dry-food diet for your cat while it is still a kitten.

This young cat uses its rough tongue to keep its white paws clean.

The more you love your kitten, the more tempted you will be to give it tasty treats. Try not to give in to the temptation too often. Is there any other way to avoid spoiling your cat? A good way to give your kitten a treat without affecting its diet is to supply it with catnip.

Catnip, which is sold in most pet stores and many health-food stores, drives most kittens wild with joy. Your kitten may play with a pouch full of catnip until he or she is exhausted and ready for a nap.

If you have a yard and you plan to allow your cat outside, then you can purchase catnip seeds and grow catnip yourself. Make sure that you plant the seeds away from flower and vegetable gardens so your cat will not disturb *your* plants. After the catnip has grown, introduce your cat to the spot. Your pet will probably take great pleasure in rolling around and lying in the growing catnip. No one is sure why cats are so fond of catnip, but you will be amused by your cat's reaction to it.

Get your cat used to dry food while it is young.

The purpose of getting to know your kitten—playing with it, petting it, allowing the occasional romp with catnip—is to win its affection. If you are successful, your kitten will begin to seek you out and follow you. It will approach you with its tail straight up and its head bowed. It will jump up into your lap for an affectionate petting, or rub itself lovingly against your ankles.

These are all signs that the kitten has agreed to be your pet. Now you and your kitten are set for a long and special relationship.

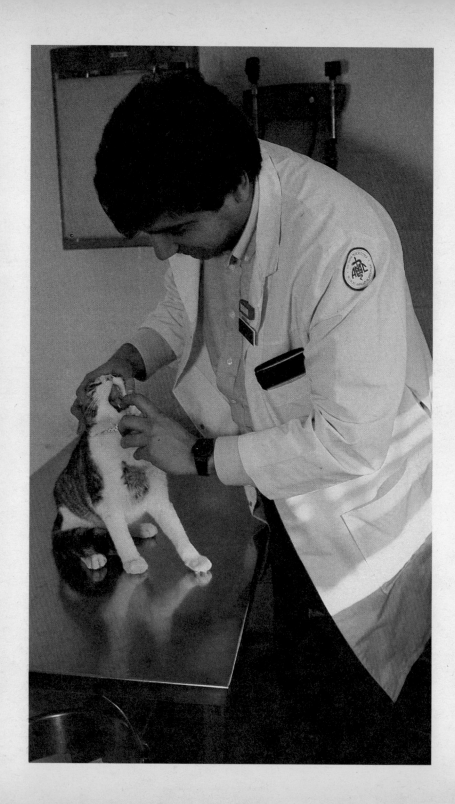

5

If Your Cat Gets Sick

Cats do get sick from time to time, so you may occasionally have to take it to the veterinarian. Most of the time you will know if your cat is ill. What are the signs? A vet should check out any of the following symptoms: frequent vomiting; frequent diarrhea; a bloated belly; runny, dull, or closed eyes; restless or strange behavior; no desire to eat; coughing or sneezing; constant scratching or head shaking; or any combination of the above.

If something is wrong with your cat, don't delay taking it to the vet. If you are not sure that your pet is sick, call the vet's office and carefully describe your cat's symptoms. Ask for a judgement as to whether the cat should be taken in for a visit.

Not all signs of sickness are as obvious as those listed above, so you should watch your cat for changes in its personality. It might lose interest in playing or become surprisingly unfriendly. If something like this continues for two or three days, you should probably take the cat to the vet for a general checkup.

When you do take your cat for a checkup, ask the vet any questions that have come up since the last visit. If your pet isn't sick but doesn't appear truly healthy to you, ask the vet if a cat vitamin is a good idea. The vet can tell you the best kind to buy for your cat.

If the vet determines that your cat is sick, then he

Have a veterinarian check your cat if it shows signs of illness.

or she will prescribe medicine and treatment. In certain cases, giving medicine and treatment may have to be done by an adult. You can discuss this with the vet and your parents.

A common health problem for cats that usually does not require a vet's help is fleas. A good time to check for fleas is when you brush your cat or when you see your cat scratching itself more than usual. An assortment of washes, powders, and sprays can be bought from pet stores. Use any one of these, as directed, and with the help of your parents.

If your cat behaves in an unusual manner—if it is bad-tempered or always tired—it may be best to take it to a veterinarian.

Flea collars are another popular method of controlling fleas, but they sometimes have a bad effect on cats. If you put a flea collar on your cat, take it off immediately if the cat becomes ill. Check your cat each day to make sure that the skin below and near a flea collar is not being harmed.

Kittens younger than three months should not wear flea collars. At that young age, kittens should not be treated with flea powders or sprays either.

You have now learned about some of the ways that your pet cat can be troubled by health problems. You also need to keep a watchful eye on your cat. Remember that you will know your cat better than anyone, and will be most aware of its ups and downs.

6

Grooming and Bathing Your Cat

Cats shed their hair year round, losing greater amounts during a change in season. You can help control the amount of cat hair left around your house by brushing your cat regularly. The hair of a longhair cat will become tangled and matted unless you groom it at least once a week. But even shorthair cats need to be brushed once in a while.

Introduce your cat to brushing while it is still a kitten. Hold the kitten on your lap and pet it affectionately. When the kitten is quiet and relaxed, begin to gently brush the hair on its back with a wire brush. Start at the back of the head and brush toward the tail. Always brush in the direction in which the hair lies.

At first your kitten may not want to be brushed. But continue to pet it gently and begin to brush again when it is calm. If you do this on a regular basis, the kitten will gradually get used to it. Your kitten may even learn to enjoy being brushed.

Until the kitten has learned to accept brushing on its back and then its sides, do not attempt to brush its belly. Kittens' bellies are very sensitive and they will react by wrestling with and clawing the brush and your hand.

Longhair cats frequently develop mats—clumps of hair that cannot be separated. To get rid of mats, use a pair of blunt scissors—those that are rounded at the tips

Get your cat used to being brushed while it is still a kitten.

rather than pointed. Cut directly into the mat in the direction of the skin, rather than cutting the mat out sideways. Cutting the mat out will leave a bald spot. Cutting into it will break it up enough so that you can comb and brush it. Be careful not to cut your cat!

Bathing your cat is not something you will have to do regularly. Usually your cat will keep itself clean. But from time to time a cat will get itself so dirty that it will not be able to do the whole cleaning job itself. The problem could be grease from a car or soot from a fireplace. In cases like these, you should give your cat a bath.

You will need help. Ask your parents or a friend to give you a hand. Fill a sink or tub with a few inches of lukewarm water. Put an old towel on the bottom so that the cat's feet will not slip and slide out from under it.

To protect your cat during a bath, ask your mother or father to place a drop of mineral oil in the corner of each eye and put a small ball of cotton in each ear.

Cats are so careful about their appearance that they even help keep each other clean.

Have your helper hold the cat firmly as you pour water over it from a cup. Use a mild soap or baby shampoo, trying not to get any into your cat's eyes or ears. Rinse the cat off, take it out of the water, and dry it with a towel.

Never bathe a kitten less than three months old, and never dunk a cat's head underwater. Only give a bath when it is really needed, because frequent baths will interfere with the normal condition of your cat's skin and fur.

Even though you will have to be firm with your cat when giving it a bath, make every effort to be kind and gentle as well. Cats do not really like water, but if they like and trust you, it may be a little easier for them to handle a bath.

7

Life with Your Adult Cat

When your kitten finally becomes an adult cat, you will appreciate the results of your careful efforts to raise it properly. The well-behaved cat eats its regular food without fuss, is friendly to you and to others, and keeps itself clean.

An adult cat often "talks," using a wide variety of purrs, chirps, meows, and cries to express many cat feelings and needs. If you pay attention to your cat's talking over a period of time, you may begin to understand these sounds.

A cat also shows its feelings in other ways. A steadily wagging tail means that it is getting angry. But when its ears lie back flat on its head, that means your cat is already angry.

When a cat's ears point forward, it is interested in something and is alert. It may be listening to the sound of a mouse in the wall or to the footsteps of someone in another room.

A cat's basic senses are all sharp. It sees, smells, hears, and tastes well beyond the ability of humans. These talents, along with a cat's excellent balance and strength, make it a superior hunter.

A cat takes great pride in its hunting ability, and the cat's instinct to hunt is so strong that you should not

It is your cat's instinct to hunt.

expect to change it. If your cat delivers a freshly killed mouse or bird to you, do not attempt to punish your cat. A cat's urge to hunt is as natural for it as running and playing are for you.

Because you feed your cat every day, it does not *need* to hunt for food. But a full stomach will not always keep a cat from the hunt. Hunting is too much fun! Of course, if your cat is always kept indoors, and no mice live in your house, it will not have a chance to hunt. But never forget to close the birdcage door if you have a pet canary or parakeet.

Another strong instinct that your cat has is to scratch its nails. Unfortunately, some cats get into the habit of using furniture, drapes, and rugs to do this. To prevent this from happening, provide your cat with a scratching post—a small log nailed upright on a square plywood base. Wrap a small piece of carpet around the log to provide a pleasing texture for your cat to scratch.

Watch your cat from the time it is a kitten. Whenever it begins to scratch on a chair or couch, pick the cat up and firmly say "No!" Then immediately take it to the scratching post. Never let it scratch elsewhere. Eventually, it will learn to scratch only at the post.

There are two situations that are particularly difficult for cats. You should be aware of how to handle both. One is travel, and the other is a move to a new home.

When you take a cat with you on a trip, much depends on how it behaves. Cats are all individuals. They react differently to different situations. But in practically all travel situations, it is best to confine your cat to a cat carrier. You can buy a cat carrier from most pet stores.

The easiest way to use the carrier is to let the cat get used to it ahead of time. A few weeks before your trip, put the carrier down on the floor and invite your cat to explore it. Eventually put your cat inside and close the door. Let the cat stay inside until it relaxes and settles down.

When you travel by car, never lock your cat—or any pet—inside the car with all the windows rolled up. For summer travel, a wire-cage cat carrier will be most comfortable for your cat.

This Russian Blue has become a fine pet.

Once you shut the lid on a cat carry-case, the passenger is never too happy. But it's the best way to get your cat from place to place without trouble.

Before traveling, always call your vet's office. Ask whether your cat will need a health certificate to travel in the state or country you intend to visit. The vet can arrange for any shots or official forms that are needed.

While travel can be hard on your cat, there is nothing more upsetting to him or her than a change of homes. Cats get very attached to places, and moving will often result in either bad behavior or running away.

Prepare for this. In your new home, keep your cat in a room with familiar objects. Give the cat a great deal of attention and affection. Perhaps give it a special treat at mealtime, such as fresh liver or kidney. Wait until all signs of nervousness and unusual behavior go away before allowing your cat outdoors.

As you can see, cats are special animals. Their keen senses and their temperament require that you be considerate, gentle, and kind. But cats are also appreciative. If healthy, they will pay back your kindness with great amounts of love and affection.

8

When Your Cat Has Kittens

Millions of kittens are born each year, but there are no homes for many of them. If your cat is a female, she will be ready to have kittens for the first time when she is between six and eight months old.

Before that time you should decide, along with your parents, whether or not you will be able to find homes for a litter of kittens. If you find that you cannot keep more kittens or that you are not sure you can give them away, you should talk to your vet about having your female cat "spayed." This is a simple operation that the vet can perform. It will prevent your cat from ever having kittens.

If you have a male cat, he will be ready to mate between the age of six months and a year. Young male cats will often wander away from home and fight with other male cats.

Fortunately, there is a simple operation, called "neutering," that solves all of these problems. The vet will be able to neuter your cat when he is around six months old.

If your female cat is not spayed and mates with a male cat, you can expect to have kittens in about sixty-three days. If you know the day that your cat mates, mark it on the calendar. Then you will have a good idea of when your cat will give birth.

Few things are as adorable as a mother cat and her youngsters.

Most female cats need nothing more than privacy in order to give birth. If you make too much of a fuss over your cat as she is about to have kittens, you might make her nervous and uncomfortable.

Both you and your parents should be watchful as the time approaches. About twelve hours before giving birth, your cat will disappear into a place that is likely to be dark and out of the way. This could be the back of a closet or underneath a bed. A good mother cat will handle everything herself. As each kitten is born, the mother cat will tear away the transparent sac that covers the kitten. Then the cat will lick each kitten and roll it around.

All of the kittens should be born within three hours after the first. Let the mother care for the kittens without your interference, but do put a saucer of milk near her so that she can take some nourishment.

If your cat is four or five days late in delivering the kittens, or if she seems incapable of giving birth, take her to the vet immediately. The vet will probably deliver the kittens surgically. This is known as a caesarean birth.

During their first week, the kittens will be helpless and their eyes will still be closed. The mother cat will want to be with them constantly. She will be very protective and will appreciate as much privacy as you can give her. At this time only you and one or two other people should intrude upon the privacy of your cat and her kittens. Move the litter box close by so that your cat will not have to go far from the nest to use it.

During the first week, your cat should eat a little egg yolk mixed with milk, in addition to the usual cat food. Starting with the second week, increase the amount of her food by three times what is normal. Continue this through the fifth week.

By the time the kittens are six weeks old, they

need two things. The first thing they need is to learn to eat on their own without nursing on their mother. The second thing they need is to be handled by people so that they, the kittens, can get used to handling. Kittens that aren't handled at this age may never learn to get along with people.

It is also at six weeks that you should begin to show the kittens to potential owners. Explain to people how carefully you have tried to raise your cat and her kittens. Ask them if they have ever raised a kitten before. If they have not, you may want to take some time to explain to them what you have learned.

When all is done, you will have helped get the new kittens and new owners off to a good start together.

After you have learned your cat's ways, and have adjusted to its moods and whims, your life together should have many rewards. You will have a purring, affectionate, but independent companion. Your cat will have a gentle and devoted protector. And the two of you will be continuing the ancient tradition of friendship between cats and people.

INDEX